AN
ARTISTDIRECTOR MEDIA
PRODUCTION

McKENZIE & MORGAN'S
PLAY WITH YOUR FOOD

KID-POWERED COOKBOOK

Kid-Powered Recipes for Children to Do "All by Myself"

BY **McKenzie Jordan** & **Morgan Jordan**
EDITOR **Charity Jordan** PHOTOGRAPHY & DESIGN **Justin J. Jordan**

TABLE OF CONTENTS

KID-POWERED RECIPES

TERRIFICALLY TASTY TREATS
SWEET GARDEN CUP............ **06**
MOUNT REDBERRY.............. **08**
FANCY POPS **10**

SUPER SWELL SNACKS
SOUR POWER PUNCH........... **16**
"A" CHEESY PENCIL **18**
HOME LIVING TRAIL MIX....... **20**

BRIGHT BELLY BEGINNINGS
MR. HOOT WAFFLES................ **12**
PEEK-A-BOO PARFAIT **14**

POSITIVE POWER PLATES
RAZZLE DAZZLE PLATE........ **22**
FISHER'S DELIGHT............. **24**
FIESTA SALAD **26**

HEY PARENTS!
Most of these recipes can be accomplished by little hands without the use of a stove or heat. Give them the pleasure of saying "I did it all by myself!" Our goal is to help you raise confident, creative children who use their personal gifts to create moments of joy and success.

MEET THE JORDANS
DREAMERS & CREATORS

OUR STORY The opportunity to be parents to these two amazing girls is the greatest gift ever. This book was birthed out of McKenzie saying that she wanted to be a "Chef Teacher" and Morgan loving to help in the kitchen. It is our way to support their passions while encouraging new talents. It is about giving them ownership in this world, a chance to shine, teaching them financial literacy, and helping them to create community. I hope next year they are not interested in Mars or Jupiter because it would take us a lot longer to figure out how to get them to outer space. But you best believe we would try.

SWEET GARDEN CUP

NAME: **KAMRYN** AGE: **3 YEARS OLD**

INGREDIENTS

- (1) Chocolate Pudding Cup
- (1) Vanilla Pudding Cup
- Chocolate Sandwich Cookies
- Gummy Worms
- Mini M&M's
- Graham Crackers

TOOLS

- Bowl
- Spoon
- (2) Ziploc Bags
- A Glass or Clear Cup

INSTRUCTIONS

1. Put graham crackers into a sandwich bag, seal tight, and crush with fist.
2. Put chocolate cookies into the other sandwich bag, seal tight, and crush with fist.
3. Combine chocolate pudding and vanilla pudding in bowl then stir together.
4. Pour crushed graham crackers into the bottom of the glass.
5. Spoon pudding on top of graham crackers.
6. Pour crushed chocolate cookies on top of pudding.
7. Decorate with gummy worms and M&M's.
8. Chill in refrigerator for 30 minutes, then serve.

MOUNT REDBERRY

NAME: McKENZIE   AGE: 5 YEARS OLD

INGREDIENTS
- Sponge Cake Dessert Cups
- Strawberries
- Whipped Cream (or Vanilla Yogurt)

TOOLS
- Plastic Knife
- Cutting Board

INSTRUCTIONS
1. Slice strawberries.
2. Put strawberries on top of sponge cake dessert cups.
3. Squeeze whipped cream on top of strawberries.

ABOUT McKENZIE
My favorite colors are pink, orange and gold. But when I turn 6 years old, black, white, and gray will be my new favorites. I am a really good reader. My favorite book is "My Friend is Sad" by Mo Willems.

FANCY POPS
NAME: **NYLA** AGE: **4 YEARS OLD**

INGREDIENTS
- Large Marshmallows
- Water (room temperature)
- Sprinkles
- Melting Chocolate
- Paper Decorative Straws

TOOLS
- Spoon
- Bowls
- Glass
- Paper Straws or Pretzel Sticks

INSTRUCTIONS
1. Push straw or pretzel through middle of marshmallow.
2. Dip and twist the marshmallow in water, then roll it in sprinkles of your choice.
3. To make the chocolate covered marshmallows warm and stir the melting chocolate. Dip and twist the marshmallow in chocolate, then roll it in sprinkles of your choice.
4. Allow to sit for 15 minutes, then serve.

☞ *This recipe requires a cool parent to help with hot steps.*

INGREDIENTS

- Nutella
- Frozen Waffles
- Grapes
- Banana
- Strawberries
- Cheerios

TOOLS

- Toaster
- Spoon
- Plastic Knife
- Cutting Board

INSTRUCTIONS

1. Toast waffle.
2. Spread Nutella evenly over entire waffle.
3. Slice bananas, strawberries, and grapes in half.
4. Use two banana slices and grapes to make eyes on top of the waffle.
5. Place strawberry slices at corners for owl wings and use Cheerios to create smile.

☞ *Enjoy with a bowl of oatmeal for breakfast or share with your little brother for an afternoon snack.*

PEEK-A-BOO PARFAIT

NAME: **BROOKYLN** AGE: **3 YEARS OLD**

INGREDIENTS

- Granola
- Peach Yogurt
- Strawberries
- Blueberries

TOOLS

- Spoon
- Clear Cup or Bowl

INSTRUCTIONS

1. Scoop two spoonfuls of yogurt into cup or bowl.
2. Place two spoonfuls of fruit on top.
3. Cover fruit with two spoonfuls of yogurt.
4. Sprinkle two spoonfuls of granola on top of yogurt.

JOKING AROUND

QUESTION: Why did the student eat the math test?

ANSWER: **BECAUSE THE TEACHER SAID IT WOULD BE A PIECE OF CAKE.**

SOUR POWER PUNCH

THE SISTER-FRIENDS

INGREDIENTS

- *Lemons*
- *Raw Brown Sugar*
- *Water*

TOOLS

- Plastic Knife
- Pitcher
- Wooden Spoon

INSTRUCTIONS

1. Roll lemons to soften.
2. Cut lemons in half.
3. Squeeze lemon juice into pitcher.
4. Use spoon to pick out any lemon seeds.
5. Stir in sugar and water to taste.

FRIENDSHIP...

Being a good friend means having fun and sharing. Sometimes we share clothes, toys, and especially nail polish. Can you guess what alphabet we all share in our names?

"A" CHEESY PENCIL

NAME: **ARIS** AGE: **6 YEARS OLD**

INGREDIENTS

- Raisins
- Bugle Chips
- (3) Cheese Sticks
- Turkey-Ham (thick cut)

TOOLS

- Plastic Knife
- Toothpicks
- Cutting Board

INSTRUCTIONS

1. Cut two small slits at one end of cheese stick.
2. Wedge a Bugle chip between the slits on cheese stick.
3. Put a raisin on the tip of the Bugle chip.
4. Cut Turkey-Ham into small squares (you may use the cheese stick as your guide).
5. Place about three meat squares on one end of a toothpick and place the other side of the toothpick into the free end of the cheese stick.
6. Repeat steps 1-5 until three pencils are complete.
7. Place the snack in the shape of the letter "A". Enjoy!

👉 *Make this snack an "A+" by serving it with Aris' favorite foods—broccoli and watermelon!*

HOME LIVING TRAIL MIX

NAME: MORGAN   AGE: 3 YEARS OLD

INGREDIENTS

- Mixed Nuts
- Pretzels
- Raisins
- Honey Chex
- Chocolate Covered Peanuts

TOOLS

- Ziploc Bag
- Large Mixing Bowl
- Clean Hands

INSTRUCTIONS

1. Add a handful of each ingredient to your bowl.
2. Mix together gently with hands.
3. Serve or store in Ziploc bag.

ABOUT MORGAN

At school I love going to centers, especially home living! We get to dress up and pretend to be big. When I grow up, I am going to go to college, get married, get a job in "New City" where Annie lives, then get my children and have a whole life.

RAZZLE DAZZLE PLATE

NAME: **KENNEDY** AGE: **5 YEARS OLD**

INGREDIENTS

- Sandwich Bread
- Whipped Cream Cheese
- Raspberry Jam
- Fresh Cut Fruit
  (Kiwi, Berries, Melons, Grapes)

TOOLS

- Wooden Skewer Sticks
- Cookie Cutters
- Plastic Knife

INSTRUCTIONS

1. Slide fruit onto skewer stick.
2. Spread raspberry jam on one slice of bread.
3. Spread cream cheese on the other slice of bread.
4. Put slices together and gently press sandwich.
5. Press cookie cutters into sandwich to make shapes.

👉 Make this plate really shine by adding a side of carrot sticks and sliced cucumbers.

JOKING AROUND

QUESTION: What type of keys do kids like?
ANSWER: **COOKIES.**

INGREDIENTS

- Goldfish Crackers
- Celery Sticks
- Olive Hummus
- Tuna Salad
- Grapes
- Apple Slices
- Pretzel Sticks

TOOLS

- Spoon
- Plastic Knife
- Ice Cream Scooper

INSTRUCTIONS

1. Scoop tuna salad into a ball and place on plate.
2. Fill celery pits with hummus.
3. Top hummus with goldfish in a row.
4. Line apple slices in between celery sticks.
5. Cut grapes in half to make caterpillar.
6. Push pretzel sticks into a halved grape to make antennas.

SISTERHOOD...

The best thing about being sisters is playing together. We play dress up, draw pictures outside with chalk, and play our favorite game "mommy and baby." We do everything together. Sister love is the best love in the whole wide world.

INGREDIENTS

- Tortilla Chips
- Spinach and Kale Chips
- Sharp Cheddar Shredded Cheese
- Monterey Jack Shredded Cheese
- Pico de Gallo
- Diced Scallions
- Spinach
- Chopped Chicken
- Salsa

INSTRUCTIONS

1. Spread tortilla chips on a plate.
2. Sprinkle all ingredients evenly on top of chips.

☛ This fun after-school snack is a creative way to use dinner leftovers. Hype up the party on the plate by adding vegetarian chili, beans and rice, olives, or sour cream.

JOKING AROUND

QUESTION: What do you call a pig in the sun?
ANSWER: **BACON.**

ABOUT KAMRYN

I love giving Mommy and Daddy hugs, watching Dora, and eating strawberries. My favorite animal is a lion. When I turn 4 years old, I'll be a lion for Character Day.

ABOUT DANIEL

My favorite movie is Big Hero Six because I love science and building things with my Legos. When I grow up I want to be just like my daddy; he is a dentist that drives fast race cars.

ABOUT ARIS

In the morning I always brush my teeth, wash my face, put Vaseline on my face and lips, get dressed, and tell my parents "have a great day at work."

ABOUT NYLA

My favorite place to visit is St. Thomas Island so that I can go to Carnival. I love watching the marching bands with my family. When I grow up I want to be a mermaid with a pink and purple tail.

ABOUT KENNEDY

I like being a kid because it's fun. I love to go on cruises with my family and to play outside with my neighbors. My favorite sport to watch is football but I like to play soccer.

ABOUT BROOKLYN

I like to read *Fancy Nancy* and watch the movie *Annie*. My favorite part is when Annie (Quvenzhané Wallis) and her friends sing "It's a Hard Knock Life."

Made in the USA
Lexington, KY
17 November 2019